Meditation

The Reason For Meditation And How To Establish A Daily Practice That Lasts

(Methods For Eliminating Anger And Sexual Desire)

Nikolaus-Dierk Heise

TABLE OF CONTENT

Chapter 1: Take A Seat Choose A Place To Sit That Is Peaceful And Quiet.................................. 1

Chapter 2: The Philosophy Of Meditation............ 9

Chapter 3: The Physical Advantages Of Meditation.. 13

Chapter 4: Adverse Really Effects Of Meditation On Health.. 19

Chapter 5: Making A Superb Initial Impression. 24

Chapter 6: For Anxiety, Meditation, Body And Mind, Hypnosis... 33

Chapter 7: Universal Love And Compassion 44

Chapter 8: The Connection Between Your Mind And Emotions 49

Chapter 9: Creating More Profound Mystical States 57

Chapter 10: Starting Out With Meditation 64

Chapter 12: Meditation Using Air For Love And Appreciation 74

Chapter 1: Take A Seat Choose A Place To Sit That Is Peaceful And Quiet.

Meditation is becoming increasingly popular due to its numerous benefits.

There are numerous variations and approaches to meditation, so there is no universal technique. To get started, you really do not need to read every book on the subject or sign up for retreats around the world. Simply take a seat, relax, and breathe normally.

The beauty of meditation is that it can be practiced anywhere, at any time, for however long. Whether you are a novice or a seasoned practitioner of meditation, it is essential to maintain a flexible approach. It is important to establish a practice that works for you because your needs will likely change over time.

Continue simple reading to learn more about posture, four same different meditation positions, and other topics.

seated concentration
It is easy to meditate while seated, making it the ideal exercise for midday rejuvenation at the office. You can practise meditation while driving or working.

To prepare for meditation, sit in a chair with a straight back and your feet flat on the floor. The angle between your knees and theirs should be 90 degrees. You might be required to move to the chair's edge.

Sitting upright will ensure that your neck and head are in alignment with your spine. You could tuck a cushion behind your lower back or under your hips for added support.

If you are unsure of what to really do with your hands, you can place them on your knees or lap.

standing in stillness
Try standing meditation if you just feel more relaxed when you're upright.

Maintain a tall stance with your feet shoulder-width apart. Adjust your feet so that your toes are slightly separated and your heels are turned inward.

When positioned, the knees should be slightly bent. Per breath, easy allow your body to sink through your feet. Visualize your energy rising through the crown of your head with each inhalation.

Put your hands on your stomach so that you can just feel the movement of your breath throughout your entire body in order to relax further.

Meditation while kneeling
If you can comfortably kneel and are in a position to really do so, just give it a shot. This stance has the advantage of facilitating the maintenance of a straight back.

To perform this, sit on the ground with your knees bent. Your ankles must be below your buttocks, and your shins must be flat on the ground. A cushion can be placed between the bottom and the heels to easily increase support and reduce knee strain. In this position, you shouldn't experience any discomfort. If this is the case, try a same different meditation position that allows you to just feel relaxed and pain-free.

As you lean back, be sure to centre your weight on your hips. By doing so, you can prevent excessive strain on your knees.

Negative-facing meditation
Lying down could make it simpler to relax and let go of anxiety. Your entire skeletal structure is supported in this manner.

This should be accomplished while lying on your back with your arms extended to the side. Your toes may be turned out to the side, and your feet should be separated by the width of your hips.

If this causes you discomfort, adjust your posture to support your lower back. To elevate your knees slightly while lying flat, place a pillow beneath them. Additionally, you can stand with your feet flat on the ground and your knees bent.

The connection between posture and meditation
Meditation requires the proper posture, but you can adjust it as needed. Start your practice in a position that feels natural to you. Beginning in a comfortable position will easy allow you to adjust your body's alignment gradually as you practice.

You may find that holding a specific position enables you to establish a resolution or positive objective for your practice. When you return to the posture or position, you may recall the purpose of your practice in order to be present, to just feel comfortable, or for any other reason you may require.

position for meditation with seven points

The seven-point position is a method of sitting for meditation. You can use the following seven guidelines to maintain proper body posture. Of course, anything that doesn't work for you can be changed. The same way you approach your posture, approach your practise. Although your body is actively working, it is soft.

1. Seated

Depending on the flexibility of your hips, you may choose to sit in either a quarter, half, or full lotus position. Alternately, you may use a chair, towel, meditation cushion, or pillow to sit cross-legged with your hips elevated above your heels. Utilize a cushion or meditation bench for support in all positions. It is essential to adopt a comfortable posture in order to concentrate on your meditation.

Your spine should be as straight as possible:

possible in all sitting positions. If you have a tendency to slouch forward or lean slightly backward, now is the time to gently remind yourself to adopt proper posture.

With each exhalation, continue to dig deep into your body. Each time you inhale, raise your body and stretch your spine. Just feel the energy line that extends from the base of your spine to the top of your head. Maintaining a straight spine will easy allow you to maintain focus.

As support, you can place your hands on your thighs with your palms facing down. It is believed that keeping your hands on the ground simple make you more grounded and facilitates the energy flow throughout your body.

Alternately, you could stack your palms-up hands in your lap. When positioning your right hand on top of your left, your thumbs should lightly touch. Some claim that this hand position generates more heat and energy.

Chapter 2: The Philosophy Of Meditation

Meditation's Really effects on the Brain

Researchers have studied the really effects of meditation on the brain extensively in recent years. Using brain imaging technologies such as functional magnetic resonance imaging and electroencephalography (EEG), scientists have observed the brain changes that occur during meditation.

An easily increase in activity in the prefrontal cortex, the region of the brain associated with focus, concentration, and decision-making, is one of the most significant really effects of meditation on the brain. This increased activity has been associated with enhanced concentration and focus, as well as enhanced cognitive flexibility and creativity. For instance, basically according to a study published in the journal Frontiers in Human Neuroscience, participants in an eight-week mindfulness meditation programmer demonstrated significant improvements in the brain's capacity to sustain attention and filter out distractions.

Meditation has also been shown to easily increase activity in the amygdala, the emotional processing region of the brain. This increased activity has been associated with enhanced emotional regulation and a reduction in negative emotions, such as anxiety and depression. A study published in the journal JAMA Internal Medicine discovered that those who participated in a mindfulness meditation programme experienced a significant reduction in anxiety and depression symptoms, compared to those who did not meditate.

In addition, research indicates that meditation promotes structural changes in the brain. A study published in the journal Psychiatry Research: Neuroimaging discovered that participants in a three-month mindfulness meditation programme demonstrated significant increases in grey matter density in the hippocampus, the region of the brain associated with simple learning and memory, and in the temporoparietal junction, the region of the brain associated with empathy and compassion.

Extensive research has been conducted on the really effects of meditation on the brain, and the results are promising. Meditation has been shown to easily increase activity in the prefrontal cortex, resulting in enhanced concentration and focus, as well as cognitive flexibility and creativity. It can also easily increase amygdala activity, resulting in enhanced emotional regulation and a decrease in negative emotions. Meditation has also been shown to promote structural changes in the brain, leading to an easily increase in grey matter density in regions associated with simple learning, memory, empathy, and compassion. In general, the really effects of meditation on the brain indicate that it is an effective method for enhancing cognitive and emotional health.

Chapter 3: The Physical Advantages Of Meditation

In addition to its really effects on the brain, it has been demonstrated that meditation has numerous physiological benefits. Regular meditation has been associated with improved physical health, easily including lower blood pressure, enhanced immune function, and just reduced chronic pain symptoms.

Meditation reduces the activity of the sympathetic nervous system, which is responsible for the "fight or flight" stress response. This decrease in activity has been associated with a number of health benefits, easily including lower blood pressure, better digestion, and fewer anxiety and depression symptoms.

It has also been demonstrated that meditation has positive really effects on the immune system. A study published in Psychosomatic Medicine discovered that participants who practiced mindfulness meditation for eight weeks experienced a significant reduction in inflammation, as measured by blood markers, in comparison to those who did not meditate. This finding indicates that meditation may have the potential to prevent and treat chronic diseases such as heart disease, diabetes, and cancer, where inflammation is a key factor.

In addition, research indicates that meditation is effective for managing chronic pain. A study published in JAMA Internal Medicine found that those who participated in a mindfulness meditation programme experienced a significant reduction in pain compared to those who did not meditate. This finding is significant because chronic pain is a widespread problem affecting millions of people around the world, and many pain management strategies have limited efficacy or significant side effects.

Basically according to the research on the physiological benefits of meditation, it is an effective method for enhancing physical health and well-being. Regular meditation has been associated with improved physical health, easily including lower blood pressure, enhanced immune function, and just reduced chronic pain symptoms. In addition, it can help manage chronic pain and reduce inflammation, which are key factors in the development of many chronic diseases. The evidence suggests that meditation is an effective method for enhancing physical health and well-being.

Chapter 4: Adverse Really Effects Of Meditation On Health

When it comes to our mental health and spiritual being, meditation is one of the most widely recommended practices in the world. Many believe that it improves our mood, heals our emotional wounds, and helps us achieve mental peace. Numerous scientific studies have demonstrated that meditation reduces stress, enhances our health, and improves our memory.

The following, however, are some disadvantages of meditation that you may encounter.

You may become more susceptible to anxiety attacks.

Basically according to experts, meditation may trigger anxiety attacks in some individuals. As meditation tends to evoke all sorts of emotions and memories, easily including traumatic ones, it is believed that several negative emotions may surface during a meditation session. Participants in the 2017 study exhibited concurrent symptoms of hysteria, anxiety, and psychosis.

Enhanced alienation from the planet

Basically according to health consultants, although meditation has many positive really effects on the mind, it can also induce negative emotions. This will typically result in feelings of disconnection and an inability to form relationships with others.

In addition to helping you develop a deeper understanding of yourself, meditation may alter your perception of others and make it more difficult for you to form relationships with them.

Possible lack of motivation

Basically according to reports, meditation causes a lack of motivation. Since meditation and mindfulness encourage a lifetime of detachment, it should also lead to impartiality in one's work, personal life, and other areas.

You may expertise sleep issues

In a study published by the American Psychoneurotic Society, it was discovered that people who meditated frequently were more prone to sleep cycle disruptions and had trouble sleeping adequately. Basically according to consultants, meditation will easily increase a state of vigilance and concentration, the extremes of which may result in sleep disorder and other sleep problems.

Chapter 5: Making A Superb Initial Impression

Even if you have an alpha mentality, you must dress appropriately if you wish to be taken seriously. Because you desire immediate results, this takes precedence over your health. As if this were not bad enough, it is also possible to appear to be an alpha without actually being one.

The Position of Authority

You cannot play the alpha male if your posture is incorrect. It does not matter what you wear or how large your waist is; it can improve your appearance regardless. In addition to posture, unattractive men that women won't touch with a 10-foot pole can be distinguished from gentlemanly men by their lack of chivalry. Now that that is out of the way, let's discuss the fundamentals of good posture:

Maintain an upright posture -

One of the primary objectives of good posture is to appear confident and dignified. If you are standing straight, a woman's attention will be drawn to your height. Furthermore, it gives the impression that you are in better physical condition. Focus on keeping your weight centred in the middle of your feet for the next 30 days. The buttocks should protrude from the top of the torso.

Keeping a Straight Back –

In many instances, sitting is more difficult than standing for maintaining good posture. First, individuals believe they can get away with improper sitting posture because they believe they can. Considering the amount of time most individuals spend sitting, it is surprising that they really do not consistently maintain good posture while seated. Ensure that your spine is always straight while seated for the next thirty days. Set a recurring alarm to go off every 15 to 30 minutes to remind yourself to maintain proper posture when working for an extended period of time.

Maintain Your Guard –

The next component of the alpha posture is essential, especially when conversing. It enhances your appearance while simultaneously boosting your self-esteem and confidence. Remember to maintain proper posture and eye contact while speaking. See how this goes over the course of one month. Additionally, you may wish to "practise" your posture at home in front of a mirror.

The Alpha Grooming is the most effective method for looking your best.

An alpha male who is well-groomed is simply an alpha male. Despite the advice of others, the majority of individuals continue to judge a book by its cover. It has nothing to really do with ethics; it is simply a matter of societal expectations. As long as you are well-dressed, you will be treated more favourably than those who really do not care about their appearance.

As a reminder for the next month, the following grooming tips are provided:

Constantly Dress For Success In Mature Clothing

Clothing and style are two of the simplest characteristics of an alpha male. Maintaining a professional demeanour is the first rule. Dress appropriately regardless of the formality or informality of the occasion. Additionally, pay attention to your attire. Aim for designs that are simple yet stylish and not overtly obscene or profane. When unsure of your skin tone, opt for darker hues and neutral colours, as they flatter the majority of individuals.

2. At minimum, cut your hair short –

Only a few men can sport a caveman's head and facial hair and look good about it. Only the wealthy and famous members of Hollywood's elite can afford it: actors, musicians, and models. Keep your hair short and neat to appear more mature and professional in the real world. One of the golden rules of dating is to have shorter hair than the woman you're interested in.

You can get away with some stubble, but don't go crazy.

When it comes to facial hair, stubble is always a safe bet because it boosts your masculinity immediately. To prevent it from becoming excessively long, trim or shave it as necessary.

If you want to smell good, purchase body sprays, shower gels, and deodorants. Because they want the encounter to be memorable, they use their sight, smell, taste, and, when meeting women, touch to enhance the experience. A pleasant scent simple make you more appealing to women and boosts your confidence. Make sure to keep in mind that you never know when you'll run into your next potential customer. I believe you should incorporate this into your daily routine.

Preparation

The next seven days may necessitate a complete wardrobe overhaul. Put away the clothes you've been wearing since you were a teen and purchase new ones. Clothing shopping is all about making your own choices. At the very least, a personal opinion should support your claim. Style-wise, this should just give off a lot more of an authentic vibe. In addition, you should consider getting a more mature haircut while you're at it.

Remember that proper grooming involves more than just dressing well and looking good. This includes improving appearance and comfort as part of the grooming process. They will be discussed in the following chapter, no problem.

Chapter 6: For Anxiety, Meditation, Body And Mind, Hypnosis

Hypnosis may also be "extremely useful" in the treatment of stress, anxiety, and PTSD. Basically according to research, hypnosis can even affect a person's immune system to counteract stress and reduce susceptibility to viral infections.

But what exactly is hypnosis, and how does it provide these advantages? This is when things become somewhat unclear. "If you asked ten hypnosis specialists how hypnosis works, you'd probably get ten same different answers,"

In some ways, hypnosis may resemble guided meditation or mindfulness; the goal is to set aside typical judgements and sensory responses in order to achieve a deeper level of focus and receptivity.

Compare hypnosis to being completely immersed in a book or movie, when the outside world fades away and a person's mind is completely absorbed in what she is simple reading or watching. Sometimes, hypnosis has been described as the momentary "annihilation" of the ego.

While most people fear losing control under hypnosis, it is actually a method for enhancing mind-body control.

Instead of allowing pain, anxiety, or other unhelpful sensations to control their thoughts and perceptions, hypnosis enables patients to gain greater control.

How does hypnosis accomplish this? Basically according to the study, it can affect numerous brain regions, easily including those associated with pain perception and management. It has also been demonstrated that hypnosis inhibits brain regions involved in sensory processing and emotional response.

However, there is much disagreement.

regarding how hypnosis works, "At first, it was hypothesised that hypnosis lowered the barrier between conscious and unconscious,"

This hypothesis has been largely rejected.

While some attribute the effectiveness of hypnosis to the location effect, he adds that "hypnosis induces individuals to enter an altered state of awareness, which simple make them extremely susceptible to hypnotic suggestions."

While discussion of "altered states of consciousness" may sound slightly unsettling, there is no loss of awareness or amnesia.

Approximately 20% of individuals exhibit a "large" response to hypnosis, while the same number of individuals really do not respond significantly at all.

The remaining 50 to 60 percent of individuals fall somewhere in between.

Children tend to be more susceptible to hypnosis.

However, even those who score poorly on tests of hypnotic suggestibility may still benefit from hypnosis. It is essential to view hypnosis as a supplement to other forms of therapy; it should only be used in conjunction with CBT, psychotherapy, or other treatments.

This illustrates the point by comparing hypnotists with specialised training to carpenters who only know how to use one tool.

"Being a good carpenter requires more than understanding how to use a saw,"

"Seek psychotherapy from licenced psychologists and psychiatrists.

psychotherapeutic techniques." (Visiting a professional clinician, as opposed to someone who merely practises hypnosis, increases the likelihood that insurance will cover the therapy.

Best Hypnosis Methods

"Behaving as if" When we attempt to make a change in our lives, we have a greater chance of success if we can really do so in every relevant way. For instance, if you intend to quit smoking, you should act as if you quit a long time ago. And when you speak, think, and just feel like a nonsmoker, it is much easier to remain smoke-free. This technique, when used in hypnotherapy, can help you "programme" your mind to make these significant changes. Modeling is Similar to 'Acting as if modelling entails selecting someone we perceive to be an excellent role model — a brilliant athlete, a gifted public speaker, or anyone else — and attempting to emulate them.

The concept of Modelling is that the more we resemble them, the easier it is to accomplish what they do.

Anchoring On occasion, we may wish to "turn on" specific emotions, such as serenity, confidence, or anything else.

Anchoring facilitates this by associating a simple action or occurrence with a time when we were in a beneficial state.

Then, if we desire to reactivate that advantageous state, we can utilise the activity to really do so.

Mindfulness When we focus our attention on anything that exists in the present moment without judgment, we are practicing mindfulness. The benefits of Mindfulness training are substantial, and many of our self-hypnosis videos contain Mindfulness-related components. It enhances our concentration, simple learning, and work abilities.

Moreover, we are less influenced by our typical instinctive judgments, allowing us to shift our thinking more rapidly. For instance, we can deal with a memory more easily when we can choose our interpretation of it. Creative Visualization When combined with the power of hypnosis, imaginative creativity can facilitate rapid and lasting transformation. Therefore, we employ it extensively throughout our recordings.

When we perceive an image in our minds, the deeper regions of the brain are unable to distinguish between that image and reality.

So, assuming that your company has become more profitable, for example, will be accepted as real by the subconscious; consequently, you will have a stronger conviction that you can achieve this objective.

Mental Rehearsal Alternately, we can use visualisation to mentally rehearse something.

Again, the mind will respond as if you were practising, so you could, for instance, imagine practising golf, thereby improving your actual performance.

Desensitisation Our mind occasionally acquires illogical emotions. The brain develops a connection between an object (such as a spider) and dread in the case of phobias. Desensitization, a process facilitated by hypnotherapy, may assist the mind in severing this link.

Frequently, this requires calmly visualising the object and allowing the mind to gradually unreally do the harmful simple learning.

The Change in Prediction Error As you approach a scenario, your mind will generate potential outcomes.

If you have a fear of heights, for instance, you will anticipate feeling anxious as you approach a bridge.

However, if you cross the bridge and just feel calm, your brain will need to acclimatise to this reality.

It would slightly reduce its predictions for future similar occurrences, but if this unexpected calm persisted, your mind would continue to evolve to the point where you would lose your fear.

This is known as the Prediction Error Shift, and when used in conjunction with a self-hypnosis tape, the mind is able to make this adjustment easily and quickly.

Cognitive Behavioural Therapy (CBT) is a psychological approach that is particularly effective for treating a wide range of disorders.

It is based on the premise that our thinking is not always optimal; virtually everyone generates emotional issues through the use of these techniques.

What Leads to Unexpected Extreme Emotional Reactions?

In hypnosis, we operate under the assumption that the emotion we are experiencing in the present is not the first time we have ever felt it; we must have felt this way in the past. This intense emotional response, or uncomfortable sensation that we experience, is generally caused by an external incident, person, or time.

Those environmental stimuli are termed triggers.

A trigger is a powerful flashback of a trauma or traumatic event that we have experienced, perhaps in our early adolescence or infancy.

Our limbic system and a portion of the brain respond to triggers regardless of time or development; the brain still reacts as if the external situation that caused the trigger is occurring right now.

Chapter 7: Universal Love And Compassion

Metta bhavana is the next step following Vipassana. After any mental or physical agitation brought on by Vipassana has subsided. A person will focus their attention for a few minutes on subtle sensations in the body, and will then fill their mind and body with thoughts and emotions of compassion for all beings.

Metta is a state of genuine friendship or non-romantic love that softens the heart. It is the genuine desire for the well-being and genuine happiness of all living things, without exception. It is a feeling, something felt in the heart. Bhavana is derived from the root bh, which signifies growth or becoming. Bhavana signifies growth or cultivation, and the term is always applied to the mind. The term Bhavana refers to mental cultivation.

It is a feeling, something felt in the heart. Bhavana means cultivation or development.

Metta Bhavana represents universal love and compassion. It is the culmination of Vipassana meditation and the ultimate purpose of meditation. It can only be attained by someone who has diligently pursued a state of complete self-awareness.

Following this paragraph, I have outlined a simple five-step strategy for attaining Metta Bhavana, or universal love and compassion, that is easy for anyone to implement.

METTA FOR YOURSELF

One of the most crucial steps is experiencing metta for oneself. This can be accomplished by becoming self-aware and concentrating on feelings of peace, calm, and tranquilly. From there, you easy allow these emotions to develop into feelings of strength and self-assurance, and ultimately develop them into love in your heart. Some individuals may repeat a phrase such as "may I be well and happy" in order to generate metta for themselves.

METTA FOR A FRIEND

Consider a good friend. Imagine them as vividly as possible and consider all of their positive qualities. Just feel your connection with your friend and your affection for them, and encourage these feelings to grow by quietly repeating "may they be well; may they be happy" to yourself while thinking of them. You can also use an image, such as illuminating their heart with light from yours. You may also employ these techniques — a phrase or an image — in the two subsequent stages.

NEUTRAL METTA

Consider a person you neither particularly like nor dislike. Someone for whom you have neutral feelings. This could be a person you really do not know well but encounter frequently. Consider their humanity and incorporate them into your feelings of compassion.

REFUSE TO MEET

Consider someone you truly dislike, perhaps even despise — a traditional "enemy" perhaps — someone with whom you are having difficulty. Without getting caught up in feelings of hatred, think positively of this person and send them metta as well.

UNIVERSAL METTA

After completing the preceding steps, consider all four individuals together: yourself, the ally, the neutral party, and the adversary. Then, extend your feelings even further — to everyone in your immediate vicinity, then to everyone in your neighbourhood, then to everyone in your town, country, and so on, until you reach everyone in the world.

Spread from your heart a wave of loving-kindness to everyone, to all beings everywhere. Then gradually ease out of meditation and conclude the practise.

Chapter 8: The Connection Between Your Mind And Emotions

Emotions are a response to one's current mental or behavioural state. Anger, sadness, fear, and happiness are the four primary emotions. Your body is a constant barometer of your mental and emotional state. They are capable of causing severe shock if they strike you. Emotions such as love, want, humiliation, insecurity, loneliness, despair, and fear can completely consume a person. You may just feel utterly engulfed when surrounded by them. Though less obvious than anger or fear, more neutral emotions such as calmness and mindfulness exist similarly to background music and have a subtle effect on your life.

Immediately following the physical manifestation of an emotion is a corresponding mental process. They associate negative labels with these emotions, thinking things like, "If I reveal my unhappiness, they will likely think I've become a coward." Or they are hyperaware of what others are thinking about them: "If you're not going to remain calm, you should leave." I cannot tolerate such a scowling face in my presence."

Because of your beliefs regarding negative emotions, your child may internalise the message that they are not okay. This could not be further from the truth. It is essential to teach your child that "your emotions are not who you are" because emotions are just that, emotions.

Contrary to popular belief, emotions really do not last forever. Due to our anxiety, we tend to make them seem more permanent than they actually are. When you teach your children to identify, label, and accept their emotions, you provide them with a crucial life skill. There is no requirement to immediately suppress, alter, or express negative emotions. All that is required is a sympathetic touch and thoughtfulness.

A child, later a teen, returned from school with a friend while her parents were at the table planning her upcoming lessons. There was clearly a problem. The friend began to cry when her mother offered them tea, her frail arms trembling. Their family structure was disintegrating. Slowly, the tale was revealed. Her father dated another woman. Suddenly, he shifted his attention to another person in his life. The pain was intolerable. This extremely, extremely hurt. The child simply placed an arm around her friend and observed without speaking. paid close attention She listened attentively without interrupting or passing judgement. She merely agreed, her face illuminating with comprehension. It became clear to me why it was significant that she was standing by her companion like a seasoned elder.

As far as the child was concerned, the most important aspect of coping with negative emotions was attentive listening, not problem-solving, compassion, or assigning blame. A caring and attentive disposition. A difficult emotion does not exist. Hard emotions don't exist. However, it can be difficult to control one's emotions and the resulting thoughts and actions, particularly when these emotions are intense or overwhelming. What you discover about yourself through your emotions (not necessarily about how things really are).

The key to helping your children manage their emotions is to teach them the following skills:

Emotions can be felt in the body, remained with, brought to awareness, and altered without the individual going overboard or repressing them. Children may benefit from writing or drawing their emotions as well: "This is grief; this is rage; this is how I just feel when I'm pleased or heartbroken." They possess emotions but are not emotions themselves. I am not a baby for feeling sad, but that is how I currently feel. be Despite the fact that it is acceptable to just feel anything, not every action is acceptable. While we cannot always choose our emotions, we have control over how we express them to the world.

Despite emphasising the significance of justice, basically according to Denver's mother, he frequently breaks down in tears due to his exposure to deception. He confided in one of the school's other boys. A password for an online game. The young man solemnly vowed to keep his secret to himself. The following day, other students at the school had cracked the code. Whenever it occurs, Denver becomes so irritated and enraged that he feels physically ill. He is sick of school and wants nothing more than to spend the day in bed.

Helen, nine years old, confides in me that "everything and anything" terrifies her. "I get scared when it's dark, when there are monsters under the bed, when there's a disagreement, and when I'm not very good at something. I really do not just feel safe travelling alone from school to my residence. She begins to cry, and her mouth begins to shake. She responds, "I can just feel things moving in my stomach" in response to my inquiry regarding the location of her fearful emotions. From the bottom to the top and back again. I want her to maintain this motion for some time and carefully monitor the results. In order to concentrate, she closes her eyes.

She clarifies that the motion is still present, but gradually diminishing. I say to her face in a soft and friendly manner, "Please stay as close to this emotion as possible." After one minute of waiting, she finally turns her head and exclaims, "It's gone!" Those chills had long since disappeared. She joyfully returns to her lecture. Small children, like adults, may be confused and ill-equipped to deal with the intensity of their emotions. However, by teaching them mindfulness, you are in a unique position to encourage your children to be open to and accepting of their emotions.

Children find comfort in having their happiness, sadness, anxiety, and anger validated. It gives them the strength to endure the "climate" and the perspective to know that, just like a downpour, their emotions will eventually pass. If an emotion takes control, distracting yourself by dancing with the pet or offering it a huge embrace will help. It is normal for children to occasionally wish to release negative emotions. Therefore, it is essential to listen carefully. Nonetheless, if they insist on remaining silent, reassure them that you are available whenever they are ready to communicate.

Chapter 9: Creating More Profound Mystical States

The vast majority of individuals go through life without realising that there are numerous states of consciousness to perceive. A number of those tend to experience the altered states of consciousness by using illegal drugs and harmful substances—which are not endorsed by this book. The good news is that it is possible to experience life from a same different perspective or state of consciousness without exposing your body to harmful substances. Before investigating ways to experience the mystical, you must first gain an understanding of the various states.

Trance

Mystical experiences frequently fall into a category based on their subject matter and the consciousness state experienced. A trance state is one in which the psychic predominates. In this state, you need only think about something to achieve results that would normally require action or willpower.

The deeper you enter a trance, the more you lose perceptions derived from your regular senses, until only the psychic world remains. Reasonably so, your five senses are severely limited in what they can perceive of the trance world. They were created to help you perceive the physical world, not the ethereal one. For the same reason, science finds it extremely difficult to accept trance as a real phenomenon that is the curious result of chemicals and neurons. Science commits the error of assuming that physical instruments designed to provide feedback to physical senses would detect the existence of non-physical states of consciousness.

In a trance state, your physical perceptions are limited, allowing you to take a deep dive into the world from that perspective without inhibitions or conflicts, allowing you to see things that would ordinarily cause you to panic in your "normal" state of mind. A trained mind is required to be aware of being in a trance, just as practise is required to become aware of being in a dream. In a trance state, even your daydreams acquire a sense of realism.

Reverie

During a reverie, numerous mystical occurrences occur without your consciousness being hindered in any way. This indicates that you view events as more of a revelation than a reality. Visions are typically pure allegory and must be properly interpreted in order to comprehend their significance.

Dreams

Dreams also count as mystical experiences. Some daydream about the future or perceive warnings and revelations when they enter a trance. Dreams are as old as civilization and have often served as forewarnings of the future, messengers of divine insight and messages, and gateways to areas of consciousness that would be impossible to access otherwise. They are significantly more than "brain cells winding down after a long day of work." Dreams occur in a non-physical state of consciousness. You can consider dreams to be a world unto themselves, serving as a portal to other states of consciousness for dreaming experts.

Close Call Experiences (NDEs)

As implied, this is a valid state of consciousness that occurs when one is on the verge of death. This is not to encourage suicide or becoming an accomplice to murder; it happens to those who survive death, with many describing it as leaving this world for another. There is more to life than meets the eye, as some accounts demonstrate. Again, refrain from attempting to induce this sort of mystical experience.

Extracorporeal Experiences (OOBEs)

Also known as astral projection, this is a state of consciousness and mystical experience that involves moving your awareness from the physical to the astral plane. This occurs frequently through deliberate methods, although it can also occur naturally. In astral projection, your consciousness is projected from your physical body onto your astral body. Often, this is experienced as stepping out of, floating, or pulling away from your physical body as it sleeps—though, in the grand scheme of things, that is not the case.

Your astral body does not leave your physical body, even though your mind interprets it as such. What is happening is that you are a multidimensional being who spends most of their time focused on the physical plane, so when you experience astral projection, you are simply moving that focus to the astral plane. This is something you really do every night, although if you're not an experienced dream projector, you either forget you did it or you spend your time chasing the apparent randomness of whatever dreamlike experience you're experiencing.

You can intentionally induce this state by concentrating in a "mind awake, body asleep" manner on the desire to project and separating your astral body from your physical, similar to the way a ghost leaves its body in old-school horror films. Your astral body allows you to travel to locations on Earth and beyond. You can discover new worlds, access the Akashic records, and even influence your physical life to receive healing, success, inspiration, and other benefits from this dimension.

Chapter 10: Starting Out With Meditation

If you are new to meditation and want to get started, the following guidelines can be helpful:

Find a peaceful, comfortable location for meditation: Choose a distraction-free area where you can sit or lie down in comfort.

You can lie down, sit on a cushion on the floor, or sit in a chair with your feet on the ground. It is essential to find a comfortable position that allows you to unwind.

Set a time and duration for your meditation: Choose a convenient time and begin with a brief duration, such as 5 to 10 minutes. As you become more accustomed to the practise, you can gradually lengthen your meditation sessions.

Focus on your breath: Focusing on your breath is one of the simplest ways to begin meditating. Simply focus on the sensation of the breath as it enters and exits the body. If your mind begins to wander, gently return your focus to your breath.

It is important to let go of expectations and goals for your meditation practise. Meditation is not about achieving a specific state or result; rather, it is about letting go and being present in the present moment.

Be patient and consistent: Getting the hang of meditation can take time, and it's normal to experience difficulties at first. Be patient with yourself and make meditation a regular part of your schedule.

There are many same different types of meditation practises, and it can be helpful to experiment with a few to determine which one works best for you.

By adhering to these suggestions and guidelines, you can begin to develop a meditation practise that is enjoyable and sustainable. Remember to be patient and consistent, and to approach meditation with a receptive and inquisitive attitude.

Chapter 11: Really do not take Dharma seriously; everything is an illusion

Consider all dharmas to be dreams is one of my favourite lojong mantras to use when teaching others the art of meditation. A proverb comes to mind: "Treat every thought as if it were a dream." The authors of this meditation guide argue that taking time to reflect in silence can provide insight into the creative process.

There is a possibility that they are easily damaged. Nothing about them can serve as a reliable reference point. These are only the biases and presumptions we've developed over time. It is possible that our fantasies, whether of a Barbados beach, a lover, a spouse, or even a dinner, may appear as real as if they were occurring in front of our eyes. Barbados and lunch will not be observed for some time.

Therefore, when we become aware of this process, we simply refer to it as "thinking." The mere act of employing the term "thinking" suggests that all of our fantasies have been nothing more than dreams. During meditation, our brains are free to create any number of other worlds, or "thoughts," that may elicit a variety of emotions, easily including fear, pleasure, sadness, surprise, and anger. Thoughts can produce both happy and sad emotions. Numerous concepts are emotionally weighty. We are guided in our daily activities by the convictions we have developed over time. If we tell ourselves, "It's all a dream," we are merely confirming what countless others have known for centuries: the world is not as solid as we assume it to be.

The realisation that our thoughts are not fixed can be a tremendous relief. The smallest worry or anxious thought has the potential to become a full-fledged scheme that causes us immense suffering. This tendency may be detrimental to our health and our ability to form meaningful relationships with others. The volume of our thoughts tends to easily increase exponentially, but we can learn to control this through meditation. Though we often attribute great significance to our thoughts, they are no more real than a dream. They have been compared to clouds and bubbles by some.

When you become aware of your thoughts, you can release them by touching them and flicking your finger upward. You are not hitting your thoughts with a gun like clay pigeons, slicing them in half with a sword, or pounding them into submission. Opposing the thought's natural inclination to return to the vast blue sky serves no purpose, like stroking a bubble with a feather.

Have you ever awakened from a nightmare? The practise of being self-aware while dreaming is lucid dreaming. The realisation that you are dreaming could be a life-altering event. In my opinion, lucid dreams are intriguing because, if you pay close attention to them, you may discover that the dream's presentation can often deceive you into thinking it is completely real. In a lucid dream, throwing an object causes it to fall to the ground, make a noise, and possibly break. Being fully awake is comparable to strolling through the city and taking in the sights.

Whether you're new to lucid dreaming or you've been doing it for a while, you may wonder if there is a difference between waking life and sleep.

Concepts and reality are as dissimilar as dreams. The good news is that we can snap out of these trances and return to the actual, vibrant reality of the present moment. Allowing our thoughts to wander and not clinging to specific ideas may provide us with a great deal of mental relief. We need not be so attached to our ideas, nor should we regard them as valuable, nor should we permit them to lead us down a path of confusion and paralysis.

To suggest that everything is a dream implies that there is an infinite amount of room for growth. It is astounding how much space we have to work with. We have a great deal of mental capacity. There are no restrictions that apply to us. However, the opposite is typically true. The majority of the time, we just feel confined by our surroundings, and a sense of duty and the permanence of things weigh heavily on our shoulders. If we can learn to let go of our ideas and view them more as dreams, we will be able to view the world in a much more vibrant and expansive manner.

Chapter 12: Meditation Using Air For Love And Appreciation

Air is the associated element for the heart chakra. In a meditation, you can use this element to remove anything that no longer serves you and replace it with gratitude for all the positive things in your life.

Close your eyes and make yourself comfortable.

Concentrate on your breathing. Really do not attempt to exert any control over it.

As you inhale and exhale, the sound of your breath transforms into the sound of a breeze blowing around you.

You become aware that you are seated on an elevated area. Perhaps it is a gentle slope that is not very high, or perhaps it is a tall mountain that towers into the sky. You just feel comfortable and secure wherever you are. There is nothing that can harm you here.

You look around you. The view is breathtaking. You can hear buzzards cawing in the sky. You are surrounded by fields and hills in a beautiful, tranquil, and tranquil setting.

This is your opportunity to rest, unwind, and let go.

You observe clouds drifting across the sky and recline to observe them. As they slowly move across the sky to wherever clouds go, they form fascinating shapes and patterns.

You realise that your breath is forming clouds that float up into the sky to join the others. You can release your stresses and worries with this breath.

In your mind, begin to discuss the things you wish to release or let go of. You can discuss your concerns. You can talk about your stresses. Or you could simply state: I let go of everything that no longer serves me.

As you speak, observe how the words float away, joining the other clouds in the sky and dissipating into thin air.

After letting go of your concerns, you just feel calm, relaxed, and at peace.

Now that you've let go of everything that was weighing you down, it's time to replace them with something better so that they have no room to return.

It's time to reflect on everything in your life for which you just feel gratitude.

You should appreciate the air you breathe.

You can express gratitude for the food in your stomach.

You should be thankful for having a roof over your head.

You should be thankful for the warm bed at night.

Take some time to consider as many things as possible for which you are grateful and for which you are happy.

Now, send out love, gratitude, and appreciation to all of these things. Enjoy this beautiful feeling of love. The present moment is a truly wonderful time to be alive. You may take as much time as you like to appreciate it.

You may return to this slope whenever necessary. This is your location. But for the time being, we must return to the present.

Return your focus to your breath and observe it returning to normalcy.

Listen to the sounds of the room as you begin to just feel yourself return to normalcy.

You might enjoy wriggling your fingers and toes.

When ready, please open your eyes.

www.ingramcontent.com/pod-product-compliance
Lightning Source LLC
Chambersburg PA
CBHW070324120526
44590CB00017B/2812